CAROLYN LESSER

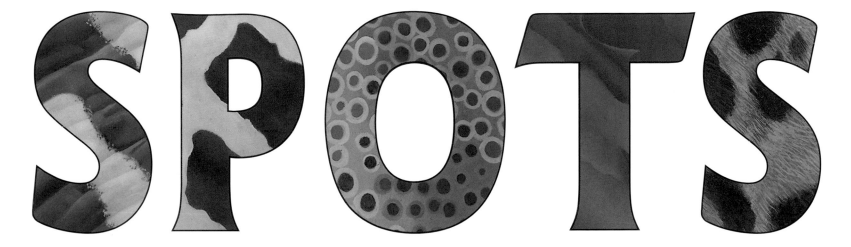

SPOTS

Counting Creatures from Sky to Sea

ILLUSTRATED BY

LAURA REGAN

HARCOURT BRACE & COMPANY

San Diego   New York   London

Special thanks to Fred Lewis, for never-failing counting help, between the lush jazz beats
—C. L.

Special thanks to Jeannette Larson, for patience and encouragement
—L. R.

Text copyright © 1999 by Carolyn Lesser
Illustrations copyright © 1999 by Laura Regan

Library of Congress Cataloging-in-Publication Data
Lesser, Carolyn.
Spots: counting creatures from sky to sea/Carolyn Lesser; [illustrations by] Laura Regan.—1st ed.
p. cm.
Summary: Spotted animals from around the world, including a leopard ray, ringed seals,
reticulated giraffes, and tundra butterflies, introduce the numbers from one to ten.
ISBN 0-15-200666-4
1. Counting—Juvenile literature. 2. Animals—Juvenile literature. [1. Animals. 2. Counting.]
I. Regan, Laura, ill. II. Title.
QA113.L47   1999
513.2'11—dc21   97-37571

First edition
A C E F D B

Printed in Hong Kong

The illustrations in this book were done in oil and gouache on Aquarelle Arches paper.
The display type was set in Goudy Sans.
The text type was set in Cerigo.
Color separations by Bright Arts Ltd., Hong Kong
Printed by South China Printing Company, Ltd., Hong Kong
This book was printed on totally chlorine-free Nymolla Matte Art paper.
Production supervision by Stanley Redfern and Ginger Boyer
Designed by Linda Lockowitz

Spotted creatures
wait for you.
Snoop and find them—
count them, too.

Flapping, looping, cruising spots...

one leopard ray

Slinking, prowling, hunting spots...

two sleek jaguars

Sunning, slipping, diving spots . . .

three ringed seals

Warming, waiting, hatching spots . . .

four cactus wrens

Staring, rippling, jetting spots . . .

five reef squid

Sloshing, wiggling, lurking spots . . .

six fire salamanders

Loping, gazing, nibbling spots . . .

seven reticulated giraffes

Leaping, nipping, splashing spots . . .

eight brown trout

Scuffling, climbing, piling spots...

nine Sally Lightfoot crabs

Sipping, flying, skying spots . . .

ten tundra butterflies

Looping one

Slinking two

Diving three

Hatching four

Jetting five

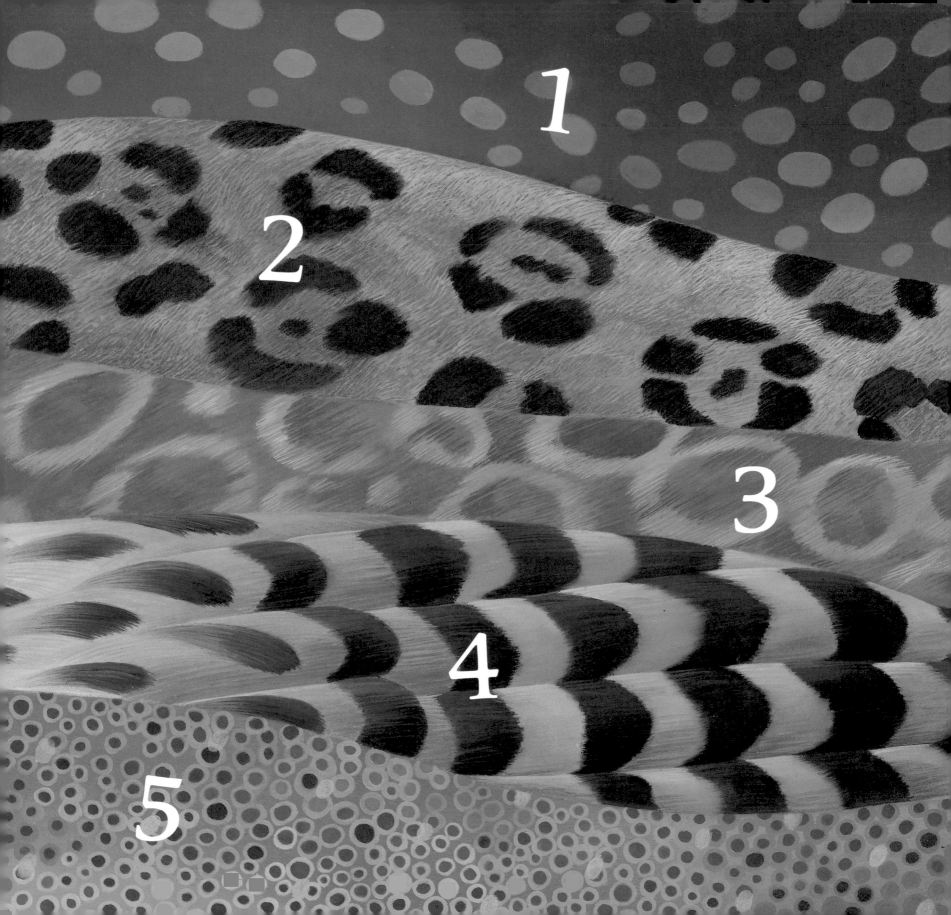

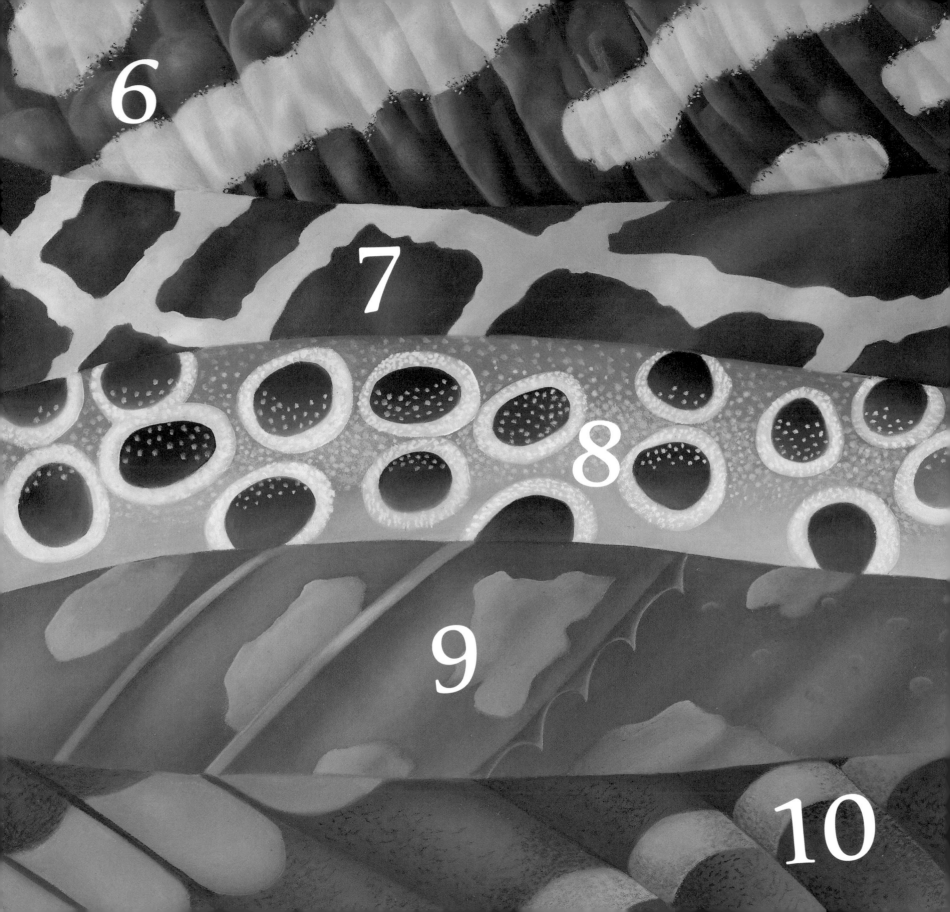

Lurking six

Gazing seven

Splashing eight

Scuffling nine

Skying ten

You can count them,
one to ten,
squid and crabs,
giraffes and wrens.

1 2 3 4 5

6 7 8 9 10

Wondrous creatures,
wild and free,
grace this earth
from sky to sea.

More to Explore

Each creature in this book lives in a different and unique **BIOME**. Scientists have divided the surface of the earth into biomes; each is a community of living organisms defined by its environment. All the biomes on the planet fit together like a global jigsaw puzzle.

Away from shore are endless **OPEN OCEANS**, flowing into one another and around the landmasses of the planet. Whales, seals, jellyfish, and plants float or swim through the oceans, and everyone is food for someone else. Leopard rays are graceful, long-distance swimmers who seem to fly underwater, flapping their nine-foot fins, leaping out of the water when chased.

The warm, rainy jungle of the **TROPICAL RAIN FOREST** is home to more different species of the world's animals, plants, insects, reptiles, amphibians, birds, and butterflies than anywhere else on earth. Jaguars are one of the tropical rain forest's big, roaring cats; fast and agile, they prowl in trees or on the ground, hunting alone.

The **POLAR** biome is made up of the southern polar ice cap (the frozen land of Antarctica, where penguins swim and dive) and the northern polar ice cap (the frozen Arctic Ocean, where polar bears hunt seals). In the Arctic, ringed seals live on, in, and under ice—basking in the sun, hiding in their lairs, and slipping into the sea to feast on fish.

A **DESERT**, created when an area receives little or no rain or snow during the year, can be icy, sandy, rocky, gravelly, blazing hot, or freezing cold. Coyotes, tarantulas, lizards, and owls burrow in the heat of the day and hunt in the cool of night. Cactus wrens build prickly-outside-soft-inside nests in cactus or thorny bushes and tuck inside during storms.

CORAL REEFS grow in warm tropical seas. Reefs are made of stony corals—animals with an external skeleton—growing side by side, over and on each other, cemented together with sheets of algae. Eels, octopuses, sea turtles, and fish hide, eat, and live in reefs. Reef squid are small, curious swimmers that usually travel in schools of five.

They appear suddenly, and as if playing a game, they swim backward if a diver swims near, and stop if the diver stops.

Trees in the **DECIDUOUS FOREST** lose their leaves in autumn. All winter, bears, porcupines, beavers, and deer hibernate or take shelter in underbrush. In spring, trees leaf and birds return, and the summer forest is never silent. Fire salamanders live in soft earth near forest streams, hiding in mud and logs during the day, slithering out at night.

The **SAVANNA** is a grassland that receives enough rain to grow trees and tall grass. It is home to herds of zebras, lions, gazelles, elephants, cheetahs, leopards, hyenas, and giraffes that hide, hunt, and graze. Reticulated giraffes eat the highest leaves of acacia trees. The silent giraffes are powerful, running fast when their sense of hearing, smell, or sight alerts them to danger.

Tall, straight, dark evergreen trees live in the **CONIFEROUS FOREST**, where winter is long and cold, summer cool and short. Bobcats, snowshoe hare, great horned owls, moose, and wolves roam the forest all year. Brown trout swim in clear streams, eating insects they find under rocks, on grasses overhanging the bank, or in the cloud of hatching mayflies rising from the stream at dawn and dusk.

COASTAL WATERS are home to mollusks, shorebirds, fish, worms, crabs, lizards, and tortoises. Waves pound the shore. High tide submerges and low tide exposes. Life thrives. Sally Lightfoot crabs are large, fast, scrambling crabs that pile on the rocky shores of the Galápagos Islands, where they pinch ticks from large marine iguanas.

In the **TUNDRA**, the vast treeless land along the Arctic Ocean, winter temperatures drop to sixty degrees below zero and high winds create blizzards. Wolves, caribou, elk, rodents, nesting birds, and insects return when spring plants appear. Strong butterflies arrive in summer to feed on nectar from flowers only inches tall. Many butterflies migrate south before winter returns, but some species remain, wrapped tight in warm cocoons nestled deep in pillowy cushions of sedge grass.